De:versify

De:versify

A Second Volume of Poems

Denny Bradbury

authorHOUSE®

AuthorHouse™
1663 Liberty Drive
Bloomington, IN 47403
www.authorhouse.com
Phone: 1-800-839-8640

Published by AuthorHouse   02/01/2013

ISBN: 978-1-4817-8316-3 (sc)
ISBN: 978-1-4817-8318-7 (hc)
ISBN: 978-1-4817-8317-0 (e)

Contents

Part IV   Human Inspiration

Part V   Love

Part VI   Other-Worldly Inspiration

For my family

and all those trying—

in whatever way they know how—

to make the planet a greener

and more peaceful place

DNIB

Also by the Author:

Poetry:

A Denagerie of Poems

Novels:

The Reunion

(A year in the lives of five middle-aged friends)

Borvo

(A ninth-century Anglo-Saxon story)

Introduction

This, my second volume of poems, contains thoughts that are inspired by the seasons, our island seascape, animals, diverse people, the oldest orders of belief, and the world as I experience it in the early twenty-first century. Our planet is full of amazing creatures and plant life that we dismiss and ill-treat at our peril. I offer these poems as a collection that reflects the often imperfect balance between humans, animals, and nature.

In the animal-inspired section, 'Horses of War' was a direct and emotional response to the stage production of Michael Morpurgo's *War Horse*. 'Realisation' (in Part IV) was a heartfelt reaction to the Haiti earthquake of 2010. In Part VI, 'Water Sprite's Happy Poem' features the joyful conclusion to one of a series of five separate fairy stories that are yet to be illustrated and published. It is included as a balance to the agony of some of the other poems. The discovery of 'the Early Poem', which led to 'A Moment Caught in Time', follows that work in an attempt to link the decades through my poetic journey.

I have lightly delved into the Japanese world of Renga. As I understand it to be it is the forerunner to our Western (clipped) idea of haiku. Writing the poem 'There and Then' was an exercise in trying to recreate an atmosphere in that tradition—and it was done with great respect for the art of another culture.

The end of the book contains a whimsical fancy about my garden nymph. As she sits there, day by day, month by month—watching and listening, I long to ask her what she knows. But of course, she will never tell!

I wish all readers joy in reading my poetry. If the metre of some is a little unusual, try reading the poem out loud in a soft, southern accent that reflects the rolling downland of the county in which I was born and brought up: Hampshire.

With respect to all poets and workers who strive for a greener world, I thank you for taking up this book.

Denny Bradbury

Part I

Animal Inspiration

Hare in the Moonlight

Hare in the moonlight,

Staring at stars.

Hare in the morning,

Hiding in grass.

Hare at his boxing,

Playing around.

Hare with her babies,

Wisdom abounds.

Hare caught in trap,

Set cruelly by man.

No escape for her—

Try as she can.

Torn to pieces

By dastardly few.

Hare was no threat.

What could she do?

Folklore suggests

Hare has second sight.

Embrace what is hidden—

Do what is right.

Hare knows the old ways;

Hare knows what we lack.

Hare sees all the mystery;

Hare keeps it all back.

We have to listen;

Find ways back to truth.

Feel out the good path—

We're gifted in youth.

Fly Free

(be not halt for me)

Halt by jess, bell and piece of rope:

Three hunters tethered

Of freedom in this misty land.

They have no hope.

People gawp around the pen—

They stare and gape—and when 'tis done,

Will walk forgetting in the sun

Proud hawk

And feisty falcon.

Eagle owl is now the star:

Wings outstretched, Nature's majesty.

Flies four yards to gather in

Day-old meat

Held out on sorry hand.

Spectacle is all they are—

Dependent on man

Who loves, but wrongly

Misguided gaoler.

Time with My Dog

My time alone

With the dog that I've known

Since he was a gangly pup.

He's majestic now,

Standing proud on the brow

Of the hill that I can't get up.

My knees won't bend;

My back's on the mend;

My mind is full to the brim.

Heart aches with the thought:

This will all come to nought,

This time with my lovely friend.

Denny Bradbury

Bees and Trees

To save the planet, we need bees and trees
Our salvation depends on both of these.
Ignoring this to do your worst:
This planet's cursed.

Gardeners plant bee friendly flowers,
Bumblebees stagger from pollen showers.
If righting wrongs is always best,
This planet's blessed.

Horses of War

Grandfathers great or great and great,
Grandmothers, too, stepped up to the plate
When the call came from over the sea.
They went or they stayed, but managed to be
All that we wanted and more—much more—
As countries of Europe went to war, damn war.

Animals too were pressed on that day
When up went the shout to march away
Each healthy horse that could give of itself
To join in the slaughterous lines of death.

They carried and pulled and charged for their lives.
They lay down without asking 'wherefore we strive?'
And died in their hundreds and thousands, and then
Most of them did not come back again.

What a debt do we owe to each lovely steed?
We offer sad thanks as they worked for man's greed.
Lessons we learned from this desperation
Should ensure that we never seek reparation.

Seagull Takes the Biscuit

Seagull sweeps in across the leaden sky:

There are rich pickings here for him to try.

His hunger drives him on to seek a meal

where e'er he can

The seaside is full of food by

courtesy of man.

Seagull is canny, wise as owl, his eyes are full of light

When he descends on promenade

he will feed tonight.

Boy drops bun, girl drops sweet, man drops piece of meat.

The ice cream is the thing he wants, and so

he swoops to eat.

No matter that it is still in tiny hand so small,

He wants it—and he'll have it

despite the sudden squall.

A cry goes up and indignation rises from the crowd,

But there is nothing they can do

as seagull's full and proud.

His chest is puffed, his feathers sleek

with oily, salty spray.

Now he struts and saunters;

now he flies away.

He will avoid the anger of those

who've gathered by the bay.

Lazy, he enjoys his triumph

he'll live another day.

Part II

Seascape Inspiration

Wave

What is a wave?

A thought from the sea,

A gift from Poseidon,

Just for me.

What is a sea thought?

Whence does it come?

Crashing about me,

Bursting through foam.

Riding the crest,

White horses charge on,

Surrounding my being,

Too soon gone.

My mind, it is still now—

Calm deep as the sea.

Watery spirit has

Quieted me.

From here I go on—

Sea thoughts and storm:

Swirling or calming,

Always perform.

Broken in Time

Sea reclaims its own
Pulling earth to drown
Sea reclaims its own
Shore has nowhere to turn.

Large boulders line the beach
Into pebbles given time
Then broken down to grains of sand
And silt and dust withal.

Relentless is the sea
Waves bring their own delight
Pounding, rounding
Pulling, thrilling
Crashing in their might.

Proud boulders that thought they were 'it'
Smart pebbles gathered en masse
Thinking safety in numbers all right.

To end as just one gain of sand . . .
Who can tell one from a clone?
Who can say I am a lone
Voice crying in the night
I above all am right?

However we perceive us to be
We will be brought down by time
We will be pounded and rounded
Until we are sand
Then we'll hear only the sea.

So Grey the Sea

So grey the sea

All white the foam

I journey forth

To come back home.

So blue and green

The like of which

I've seldom seen.

Such energetic

rolling foam:

it ill behoves me

then to moan

about the world

the state it's in—

greed and lust

of bankers' sin

who take, take, take

without remorse

then take a million

home, of course.

De:versify

it's what we're due

we've worked so hard

just thank us when

in your back yard

that's full of weeds

no time to plant—

you're holed up in

a prison hard

work pays you know it's true

that's why we're

always there

for you.

We lend you sums

if you are good

we'll let you pay back

with your blood.

Don't moan to us

if fate steps in

the roundabout

of life will gain

momentum then

who loses grip

will fall—and into

mire will slip—

we'll look down

upon the place

where you are struggling

now to face

penury and social cuts.

It's like we said:

The world's gone nuts!

Just pass the champers

Cheers, you plebs!

I mix now with

Jules and Debs.

Forget my roots

Now that's a laugh

My old Mam

Took washing in—

She scrimped and saved

For me to be

A caring bastard.

Yes, that's me.

My Dad worked on

From morn till night.

It broke him.

Now Jack, I'm all right:

They're dead and gone.

But me, I'm here.

No one will take

What's mine,

D'you hear?

I won't go back to

Where I'm from.

It's in the city

I belong.

I'm clever, too.

They all said that.

'Tis pity though,

that when it's done

I'm not invited

To the sun.

So grey the sea

All white the foam

I journey forth

To come back home . . .

Idle Tides

Shiny suit sloughed off, replaced with tartan shirt.

White legs sit dangling on the prom.

Stones thrown at other stones will never hit.

He might say that he got one that time right enough,

But how can you tell when all pebbles look the same?

Rolling, dancing, bouncing all ways—

Not quite reaching sea as waves seek the shore then back away.

Thin-legged girl sits, awkwardly aware of her paleness.

Gawky and shy, concerned only with her image.

Gradually, she relaxes and joins in the stone throwing.

Dad encourages, and they throw stones and laugh together.

Temporarily, they forget Mum, who is somewhere else—

Probably on the Costa Brava with her new man.

Does she remember the simple times of running and laughing with them

On the beach?

Bronzed Adonis reaches out for his iced drink as he shades his

Crêpey eyes from the sun with designer glasses.

She looks at him and wonders how she came to be so far away from all

she cherished,

Then reality floods in. She remembers how she was ignored and put upon.

Was that really enough reason to leave and abandon her child

And her childhood sweetheart, and her own deep unhappiness?

Purposely Drifting

Drift in time and space as the waves ripple over your soul;

Stir up the elements with a light hand and

watch the gentle lapping on the shore.

Dig not deep unless you are ready for the silt

That will inevitably surround your idyll and drag you into its depths—

But then the deep consciousness of your being

may find long unanswered meaning

In the mud:

Glory in the revelations.

Silt will settle,

Still water will flow once more

In its own time.

Inner calm will be your amazing strength.

World says:

Turning, ready or not!

Sea Changes

What changes?

What changes have you seen?

What changes what you see?

Are we altered by events,

Or do we meet headlong

Those who come to us each day

With hurts so gruesome that they seek

Help in such different ways?

Some pray,

'Is someone there, please tell?'

Some fight

And punch their way through hell.

Some cry their tears

But see no good in humankind at all—

While others learn to laugh and sing,

Make merry till they fall.

Me, I walk along the shore—
Stare at the sea and smile,
Fling wide my arms and turn about
For fully half a mile.
While breathing in the wholesome air,
The waves come up to greet me.
They fizz around my naked feet
Then run away so sweetly.

My cares are gone,
And I can face the world again
With pleasure.
Sea's never still;
It comes and goes
And soothes with equal measure.

Part III

Inspiration from Nature

Stars Tonight

I looked up and saw stars tonight; they were so bright and clear.

What is up there, I don't know, but this I hold quite dear:

That all is well as long as they are shining in my sky.

The velvet cloak of night enfolds while all I ask is why—

Why does humankind not follow the zigzag paths of youth

To find the answers to our quest for some forgotten truth?

I looked up and saw stars tonight, which is all I need to know—

That while they shine and hold their place, we have a chance to show

How we can best serve out our time on this good earth so blue.

It isn't only up to me . . . it's him and her and you.

Beleaguered by our threatening to upset the yin and yang,

Nature's balance in disarray, we must do all we can.

I looked up and saw stars tonight as sleep eluded me.

On distant stars, I pondered on what elements might be.

What don't we yet know? How we yearn to fill in all the blanks,

But it is how we deal with these that keeps me coming back

To why we are and how the wise just offer up their love

With constancy and honesty—how much our lives improve.

I looked up and saw stars tonight, then one fell through the sky.

What power I can only guess, sends light to feast the eye.

To sit and ponder in the night, to think and hope and pray,

So that we might be happier at the opening of each day.

We are so small against this web of infinite space and time.

Some look and note the fact of it while others make a rhyme.

Kingcup and Friends

Kingcup, forget-me-not, dead-nettle white:

Struggling, reaching, searching for the light.

Clover, daisy, dead-nettle pink.

Look at us,

Hear us,

Let us make you think.

Colt's foot, cowslip, white nettle dead.

See green, see blue, then see red.

Arid, treeless hedgerows bled.

Ragged robin,

Timothy,

Put us in your head.

Agrimony, garlic, rose hip, haw:

Blackthorn, convolvulus, we need more.

Nightshade woody, deadly, too.

Bumblebees,

Butterflies,

Humble shrew.

Elder, oak, birch, broom, and ash:

Let us fell and sell the lot for cash.

Campion, companion, scented pine,

Hazel,

Gorse bush,

Not yours, nor mine.

Owners not as we survey

What centuries have brought today.

Guardians of each changing mood:

Meadow,

Lea,

Deep, dense wood.

Meadowsweet, silver birch, chestnuts red:

Lavender provender, hops for your bed.

Room for all, there's room for more.

Love and leave—

Glory,

Nature will restore!

Wisdom of Trees

What does the tree know,

Leaves a-falling?

What does the tree know,

Standing there?

What does the tree know,

Leaves a-golden?

What does the tree know,

Standing there?

Eleventh hour of the eleventh month—

Cloudy, gloomy winter day.

People stop and stand and shudder,

Think of what might be today

If others hadn't gone for fighting,

If young and old alike were here

To tell the tale of war, destruction,

Greed, and violence—mortal fear.

Why can we not learn from our past?

Why can we not refuse to bear

Arms? Walk in peaceful union?

Instead we mourn—shed bitter tears.

I'll tell you what the tree knows yonder;

I'll tell you what the trees must know.

They know that given more millennia,

We still will fight from righteous outrage.

We will not give an inch and so

We needs must go through endless carnage—

Infinite in its unblessed rage.

We do not want to learn forgiveness;

We stay forever in our cage.

Yet trees will reach their searching branches

Up into the wind and rain—

They live and die as nature dances.

Next year they grow and live again . . .

Lost Meadows

Light-flooded meadows: brimming with sweet, honeyed flowers,

bedappled with dew.

Butterflies, bumblebees, damosels too drunkenly stagger

in nectar-filled hue.

How can this image today be expressed as fields drunk with pesticides

only are dressed?

Mistakes of the past rear up now to haunt us as we pass by blindly,

ignoring the facts

For so long around that we look (but don't see) how commerce has left

barren acres of tracks.

Many have now seen the light and are planting wild flowers seeds

right next to the wheat.

Bumblebees, butterflies, damosels sweet, fly up and around in

blissful nectar retreat.

We all have been guilty by absence, design, or merely a shake of

the head in resigned

Acceptance of what the men in dark suits were planning to plant next to

burgeoning shoots.

Be it wind farm or pylon—or merely a road—we sighed and we tutted

but never did goad.

Now, as we look with fresh eyes, do we see the reinstatement of the

humble and wonderful bee.

Winter Soul

Crisp, clear air of deepest winter,

Sky streaked so with pastel hue:

Dig into my soul with icy finger,

Make my heart with leaden blue.

It is all that I can muster,

It is all that I can do—

Make each day the alter ego

Of this world that's hurting too.

One more step and I can finish

What I started years gone by.

That is, love each one so dearly

That the thought leaves tears I cry

(Slowly sliding down my cheek,

Down to drop from humour still,

Down to mingle with the dust mote,

Down to clatter with the rill).

Water gathers, always seeking,

Garnering endless questing set

Fair to offer food for thought,

Safe harbour for a thousand yet.

Ice forms to make the access harder,

Icy fingers still entwined

Cold around my heart—so yearning

Warmth will ever make it thine.

Poem for February

It sits astride the seasons, riding into spring.
Dull January slips on by—cold, wet wind and rain.
March has yet to offer the hope of warmth to come.
So February makes the most of fires within the home—
Fires that come from baking cakes and puddings piping hot;
Fires that surge right through us, contentment is the rot.

We want to curl up with a book given to us by our kin,
To celebrate the winter when all go carolling.
We shiver at the thought of frost and snow and ice, it seems,
Then rush out to go skating on the deeply frozen streams.

Earth gives up and stays asleep, renewing what it lacks
By keeping still and guarding while composting gives it back.
All must be patient, must embrace the sleeping month until
Shoots break through and burst with joy as we know they will.
Cycle of the seasons: round and round and round.
We will renew as they do, if we just stand our ground,
Try not to order everyone and everything for gain.
Our perspective is so tiny 'gainst the mighty wind and rain.

Waiting for Blossom (I)

Cold sun rises each day

But brings no warmth

Winter is hanging on

Clutching at hope

Drawing us back to the long

Dark nights of shivering

Longing

Spring winds have come and gone

All is quiet calm but chill

Skin and bones

All need the longed for respite

Hawthorn is late this year

February bees come in March

Eyes that long searched for colour

Now see the wonderful hint of blossom

Soon it is everywhere

Brilliant white of blackthorn

Champagne pink of cherry

Dappled rose of apple

All framed by nature's green

Bringing gladness and smiles

Birds nest and sing their sweet notes

Pounce on the awakening insects

Jauntier walking slowly savouring

Glorious

Delightful

Burgeoning

Amazing

Intricate

Wonderful

Blossom

Joy

Waiting for Blossom (II)

Feast eyes on the abundance of colour

As it draws you into its depths, then

Seek not to stay there. For once entangled in its

Profusion, there will be a debt to pay for such beauty.

Your mind will turn in on itself and weave a thread

Known only to the spirit of the blossom.

Your world will become subject solely to the colour of light.

Turn away!

Turn away, turn quickly,

Before the spell is cast.

Let your eyes dwell on the dun and mundane.

Now spring is here, there is no need for such heralds to linger.

Let us go on knowing that next time we will be

Taken in by the breathtaking spectacle and be just

As susceptible—but the colour of the earth and the

Tender green will save us. For we must not dwell

Only in the spectacular;

The commonplace also has its say.

there and then

mist hides rising sun

people lost has day begun

birds chirrup long song

fields beckon where crops must grow

come till wave arms scare black crow

back bent over no pain

face away from driving rain

raise face sun again

smog clogs cityscape

traffic noise terrific din

weakly sun peeps in

working men and women too

onto treadmill two by two

evening moon shadows

eerie space between home blocks

eat drink watching clocks.

Gossamer Green

Gossamer tablecloth covering green,

Tiny creatures never to be seen.

Gossamer threads weaving over all,

Holding early dew in autumn's thrall.

Who ordered beauty like this to be?

Who claims the ultimate mystery?

Little eight legs, busying time—

Eyes ever watchful, waiting for rime.

Frosty mornings when winter is here,

Now to go burrowing, Hard Jack is near.

Gossamer napkins scattered and left—

Summer no longer, leaving bereft,

All those who revel in warmth of the sun;

Dying for living, the cycle is spun.

Part IV

Human Inspiration

Time and Place

What is this time? What is this place?

How do I find the friendly face that wants to meet and greet and say:

'Did you enjoy this lovely day?'

How do I go and find the one who'll listen when the day is done?

Where must I be to realise that all I want is here,

Not there?

Is it my failing not to see

That what is meat and drink to me

Is all to you? For well you know the commonplace,

The bitter blow.

If I'm to see my true reward:

Companionship, loving regard with due respect—

And this is what I do expect—

Then more than this is what I do to show compassion,

Loving, too.

My Granny said so many things.

This one I do remember well: 'Cast your bread out far and wide,

Then it shall be returned to you

Tenfold or more for

Peace inside.'

Tears

Wind whips tears to her eyes—
Wet they fall over lined face.
Weather responsible for them all.
Was it the cold or fall from grace?

Steeling herself to remember,
Stumbling on, she thinks it through.
Still in the autumn whirl of leaves,
Silence gathers, doubts renew.

Family give what solace they may;
Friends are distant, little to say.
Familiar the feelings of distress;
Foolish to worry for long away.

Denny Bradbury

Garden Fete

Around they go with fervour, whipping up the crowd.
They are committee members, resplendent and quite loud.

They need a good show this time; last year's was spoilt by rain.
No cloud can bring this show down—suns out, all's well again.

Drink beer; eat free-range burgers, pancakes, and candyfloss.
Cake stall, it is resplendent. Teas—serve scones at a loss.

In the centre, ringed by straw bales, dogs pull and scratch and chew.
Do they look like their owners? Sad truth, they really do!

Next on in the arena: majorettes with batons, twirly—
They throw them up and drop them . . . then giggle rather girly.

The silver band has come once more, a welcome bright tradition.
They play away under the trees, the tunes all old renditions.

De:versify

Scarecrows are dressed in Granny's lace, Granddad's old hat askew;
Mum wondered where her red skirt went, it really was quite new.

Small children in their fancy dress mill round and hope for glory;
Princesses mix with Beanstalk Jack—all from their favourite story.

Hook a Duck or Splat the Rat, Tombola, take your chances.
A friendly groan goes through the crowd: here come the Morris Dancers.

Once more, the bunting's put away—chairs, tables, that's the lot.
It's been the same for year on year: all fun, hard work forgot.

Denny Bradbury

A Moment Caught in Time

Old papers sifted through, long forgotten texts—
Letters from pen pals, address book littered with deaths.

Amid the sad detritus

Of a life only half-lived,

From an early poem

Seeps new hope, new breath.

It seems I was lonely as a child;

It seems that I was a poet.

Even so, I loved the downs

And trees, but didn't show it.

I learned to hide what it was I felt,

Keeping love and hopes enchained.

I learned that passion badly spent

Would leave my spirit maimed.

I long for that child, so keen.

I long to be given that chance.

I long to be what I have not been—

I long to sing and dance.

Let out that passion so long held in;

Let out the heartfelt cry.

Bring on that life I might have led;

It's never too late to try.

Denny Bradbury

Early Poem

Approximately 1963

From My Bedroom Window

Atop the hill, there stands my home,

Where I return when day is done.

And often there, I stand alone

And let my eyes around me roam.

Away to the east, the rolling downs;

Away to the south are the forests;

Away to the west, a meandering town;

Away to the north, the farmlands.

A hare sits preening her face on a mound.

The birds fly over the trees and land;

The leaves come twirling and twisting round

While farmhands work the farmers' land.

The grey stone cottages up on the downs;

The many trees clustered in rounds;

The cat, the dog, the bird and the tree—

Form part of this landscape . . . and part of me.

Withdrawing

I feel I am withdrawing from the world,
I feel the need to shut all people out—
Except that is the very inner hub,
Those who complete the circle of my life.

All others seem to hurt and sneer,
Humiliate the person that I am.
Who am I, anyway, that they should flaunt
Their cruelty to denigrate this woman?

Why should I give them time of day,
Or 'hello' in a friendly manner?
Their ridicule cuts deeper than they know,
Causes me to falter, blush, and stammer.

I am right back in classroom J—
Our teacher always tardy, yet to show.
The class bully picks on me to say
How frightful my whole being is to know.

Back then, I know not where to turn.

Can they all be in on this humiliating game?

Will no one tell the girl to stop?

Where are my champions, all the same?

But no, the bully has the floor.

I squirm and redden as they flay;

I try to turn and look the other way.

But always in my face is where they stay.

Now, as then, no one speaks up.

But now I am a stronger kind of girl,

A woman who has learnt through time

To smile, stare back, let her lip curl.

This group of women who witness my fall,

Were they the same from long ago?

I shall not let their weakness be my gall;

Rather, will pity that they have not learnt at all.

Four O'clock

When it's four of the clock in the daytime,
Then people think of tea—
Well the English do so, anyway
(And especially if they're me).

Ritualistic, calming measure:
The scoop, the pot, and cup.
Quiet place to drink in
Sunny, sheltered sup.

It's Catherine we have to thank.
From Braganza did she come,
And brought her love of teatime—
It made her feel at home.

But when that four o'clock comes—
And morning's yet to break—
It's the agony of mind
That keeps us wide awake.

Those distant sun-filled memories

Of tea upon the lawn

Drive us mad with fever

As we wait upon the dawn.

With what demonic pleasure

Do the night elves sit and wait

To curse you with each measure

Of the seconds on your plate.

No crumb of comfort do you find

In such an early feast;

Sadness at the heart of things

Feeds still your yearning beast.

Poor comfort, then, in rosy lea
That lends the day such grace.
Night-time belies the very state
That fills your daytime space.

Yet night is often when our
Darkest thoughts come home—
They're sorted into status;
By morning they are gone.

Denny Bradbury

Realisation

How cosy in my scented bath,

How warm I am and needed,

Loved, and cosseted.

Fussed and dressed—

This is one kind of reality.

This is a life.

I moan, of course, about unnecessary

Draughts.

Were you born in a barn?

Well then close the door.

Pictures in my head of what I long for:

A different life where less is more

And nature comes right in.

How wretched is this when I see

Haiti's devastation.

Am I the only well-read one who knew

So little of them?

Where did their poverty-stricken lives

Get hidden in the plethora

Of find, lock up the bad guys?

Has our team won or lost yet?

Don't spare me things I need to know—

You journalists have made it so.

You could have told me . . .

How else am I to know how people live and die?

I can't make every nation fit

Into my journeying

(Split

As it is 'twixt coast and moor,

Downland and river).

So the poor

Will wait upon my wish to know

Of other hidden depths of hell,

Where wretched creatures try to dwell

Whilst waiting for our hounds of news

To stumble blindly on and choose—

To let us know,

Then feed our muse.

So shocked are we that hands so soft

Dig deep into our souls and pull

Out sympathy and meagre change.

The lowly sous will make no dent

In bank accounts that never rent

Asunder. For

If we gave all,

Then we'd be poor.

What use is that to those who starve to know that we are also shriven

By hunger, cold, and thirst so driven

That revolution is the key

To save our souls from tyranny.

A broken nation is no good—

Deforestation and no food

Does not sit lightly on the heads

Of dignitaries come to spread

Feelings of goodwill charity.

Dispel alarm, restore the order.

Insurrection on the border

Makes uncomfortable headlines.

We squirm and wriggle in plush chairs,

Reach for bottled mountain air.

Refined and safe, we dare to care.

How soon will World Cup fever push

The poor from off the page?

De:versify

How soon will politicians fight

Each other in their rage?

How soon will we, as caring types,

Forget the distant poor

And concentrate once more on things

That batter down our door?

Immigration cultures strange

That make us feel uneasy.

Celebrities who do nought,

But dare to smile in camera (caught

Out in a fancy

For a drink or drug-crazed rant).

Give space to those who think that Kant

Is what we look for in our days,

To make some sense of modern haze.

I can't think that the world's benighted

Care one fig for who's got knighted,

Or who is kissing whom again,

Or when will sun fight off the rain.

We know of nothing worse than that:

Our neighbour shouts to stop the cat

From digging up his dahlia bed.

Crowded trains and sullen faces

Give rise to anger vitriolic.

We stumble past the alcoholic

Who sleeps in urine-sodden cardboard,

His only friend the mangy mutt

Who shivers with him

In his rut.

Mass destruction on a scale

Can only be our winter's tale

Of ignorance and blind-eye-turning,

While desperate folk die in yearning—

Twisting, agonising,

Hopeless, helpless, gut-wrenching longing.

Lothario/Lotharia

Scant hair slicked down in Brylcreem style,

Grey sideburns point to leery smile.

He sucks his teeth, then moves to show

He knows the game is played out slow.

His object is younger by far—

Ten years or more divides the pair.

She is petite if slightly wrinkly,

Silver coiffeur with eyes all twinkly.

Her last beau died in tragic circs;

He tried so hard to make it work,

But she, demanding ever better,

Dumped him with a Dear John letter.

She's now on to pastures new,

This lifelong habit is part of Prue.

Lothario will feel the rap,

Pick up the tab, and take the crap.

She will walk carefree and flighty,

And break another old heart nightly.

Another man will fall beside

The road she treads, it's very wide.

In fact, it needs to be like that:

With bodies strewn, so sad a fact,

They all want more than she can give.

Her first was just who made her live,

But he, the rotten scoundrel, did

The dirty with her best friend Syd.

Now it's she who rules the roost;

The rich and dead give her a boost.

She lives the life, that's all she can—

She only wanted one good man.

But that was never meant to be;

Her life was set by family tree.

Mother wasn't all that bad,

But then she'd never known her dad.

All the while, both mum and daughter

Set the bar and watch the waters—

Take their lives and drift on by,

They sigh, they smile, but mostly cry.

Prue's love was cunning, slid aside,

Took what he might, but not as bride.

Left her to make all others pay;

She's rich but sad to her dying day.

Man at Bus Stop

Man tying his shoelace:

Precision is all.

Oblivious to others,

He ties bow so small.

Pulling his sock up,

He pats into shape.

Dressed all in denim—

From ankle to nape—

Woman right by him,

Sits staring at space.

She's also too busy

To notice his face—

A face full of tension

That must have regard

For the tiny minutiae

That forms his façade.

Clipped movement,

Tight body,

His autistic mien.

One day, he will break,

And with tears

Will it rain.

Frustration pent up,

So long in his thrall,

Will burst like

The first flood

Diminishing all.

Still he measured

And measured

Till all it was neat.

From his hair cut,

His shirt front,

Down, down

To his feet.

Along came his bus,

Then without backward look,

He got on,

Sat still,

Woman forsook.

Not Diminished

I'll climb that hill tomorrow.

'Oh I did that yesterday;

It was easy and not worth the effort.'

Sadly, I limp away

I'll walk that road tomorrow,

When I'm fit and raring to go.

'I did that last weekend with Grandma,

Although she was rather slow.'

I really will climb that old mountain

When my leg will do what it's told.

'That old thing really was no score—

I think I was just 6 years old.'

Don't stamp on my aims and ambitions;

Don't tread me down into your mire—

I won't only fight my afflictions,

I'll fight you as well and inspire

Others who want to climb mountains

And hilltops and places remote

(That live in their hearts as a mission

Against overwhelming 'no votes').

Don't diminish my dreams with your boasting—

One-upmanship never sits well.

We fight what we must in our own lives;

Detractors can just go to hell.

Now that would be a journey to boast of—

That would be a way to gain space

In the annals of mighty achievers.

There they are in the lowliest place.

Part V

Love

My Gift to You

The discontent of winter

Lies heavy on your brow;

The eyes once full of summer sun

Shine solemn, wistful now.

You yearn for warmth and sunlight,

You long for birds to soar,

You look for buds to open

As they wake from frosty hoar.

Oh! Love is summer, it is spring—

But love is winter, too.

Be happy in the tide of life:

My love, my gift to you.

Sir Galahad

Sir Galahad, Sir Truly Great,

We are bound with love and fate.

Your story starts—six decades lost—

On stormy seas your life was tossed.

Safe harbour seemed outside your reach,

But now your boat's safe on the beach.

The tide has turned and waters flow,

Happiness is the here and now.

Forever and More

Say love is forever,

And we shall not part.

Say love is our destiny,

Our meeting of hearts.

When trouble leaps in,

We shall be like glue—

You joined to me, and me

Bound to you.

Summer Cold

Summer cold reflects your thoughts:

Dark and dank and all of nought—

Save that the sun will never shine

While he refuses to be thine.

Dreary days and colder nights,

Clouds hiding all the glorious light

That you know is there above.

If only you were as the dove,

Then you could soar into the skies

And fly forever while your eyes

Feast on the life affirming sun

And only come back when you're done.

While you are chasing clouds away,

Then other mortals, too, could play

Below in rustic idyll fair,

Bucolic merriment so rare.

Lovers, by chance, would stop and meet

While rain kissed puddles at their feet

Reflect the glow their passion sends:

To shine such warmth and make amends

For all the bleak and restless minds

Who merely wait for someone kind

To greet and smile—let love be true—

Life will seem better, rosier, too.

Hold Me Gently

Hold me gently,

Rock me deep

Into the fathomless pool of a deep, deep sleep.

There let me be till the sun reappears

And the heat of your love in the day

Dries my tears.

Tears come unbidden—

They swell up and spill

Down my cheeks to fall softly in space.

Random drops of my fears

And my loneliness

For none to see . . . as I am alone

Without you beside me.

Another Year

Expectations running high,

They plan a New Year party—

Sifting the throng for people who

Engender laughter hearty.

Time draws near, and guests arrive

With bottles, chocs, and frozen faces.

Putting age-old jokes through party paces,

All smile and go on through to eat,

Drink, and be merry in the heat

Of fire blazing, fairy lights,

Candles giving off their scent,

The talk of wonder where last year went.

Among the crowd sits one alone.

She longs and aches to be at home,

Where her dear Sidney breathed his last.

She knows he's there, his spirit's fast

Become her daily treat

As she puts up her tired feet

Upon the stool that he restored

To stop himself from being bored.

He never did like jolly 'dos'

Where his opinions were eschewed.

He was out of time and sync,

But all the same, he made her think.

He made her laugh and cared so much

About the stuff that's out of touch

With modern ways and thoughts. And so

It really was his time to go.

Lack of respect for history's chimes

That tolled relentless warning rhymes

For all to hear and see and learn.

They didn't, so it was his turn—

He went with fading heart and mind.

Loving her, he'd been so kind

To see through her abnormity,

A loving soul with empathy.

Sisters (II)

Sisters are a lovesome thing.

I've written that before,

But now, as age engulfs us,

I love them even more.

At times, they can be scratchy.

They rant, and then they fizz,

But calm will overcome them—

And that's the way it is.

They send long-distance hugs

To warm you when you're down;

They chide you and correct you

When logic's upside down.

We live our lives on different paths—

Exist on different planes—

But hurt my sister, you hurt me . . .

It's always been the same.

Belonging

Belonging is cocooning—

It makes us feel alive.

No need to fret;

No cause to moan.

Take solace enough,

Then face the world alone.

*   *   *

Belonging

We are born into belonging;

We are meant to be as one.

*   *   *

Belonging

Full fame and worldwide acclamation—

A modern sickness, no rewards

Except the sound of empty phrases

Echoing to some strident chords.

We need to feel that we are loved,

Belovéd by our guiding star.

Belonging is another measure,

Reaffirming who we are.

*   *   *

Belonging

Even to one person's pleasure—

Solitary,

Selfish, selfless,

Single-minded.

Belonging to both time and space

Only when we fully honour

Nature's smiling honest face.

Do we really fit the planet?

Dying, leaving ne'er a trace!

*   *   *

Part VI

Other-Worldly Inspiration

South Korea, Taebek Mountains. I discovered

profound spiritual peace there.

Guardian Angel

I close my eyes to find him
Walking through the trees,
Sunlight dappled on the path,
A cooling, healing breeze.

I reach the gate at lane end.
There I have to stop,
Lift the latch with solid sound—
And then I let it drop.

Walking on I see my goal:
The house of knowledge
Like my soul,
It is pure white with many rooms.
I enter and therein so soon,
My guardian angel comes
To meet me with hands
Outstretched to mine.
I stand half in the ante room
'Twixt dark and lights that shine—

They shine so with such brilliance,

That is all I see.

If only I could move on in,

But something's stopping me.

I hold the hands as offered;

He gives me gifts galore.

It's wisdom that I seek,

And I receive so much and more.

Then still not entering into light,

I turn and walk away.

Reluctant to let go the hold,

This angel holds my day.

He's always there whene'er I ask—

He'll never cease to care—

I know not who he is or why,

But I'm happy that he's there.

Back through the gate with pleasing latch—

Back through the woods so calm—

My eyes are full of tears but yet

Life is now smoothing balm.

I have been soothed,

I have been given

Peace amid the storm.

I am so blessed with this great gift

Of wisdom with the dawn.

Spirit (H)

Oh Spirit who or what are you?
Why do I need to know?
Why do I need to pin you down
Your truth and form to show?

It is enough that you are there
To guide me on my way,
To help me make decisions
With the breaking of each day.

Depending on the right of it,
Dependent on the course,
Defending all decisions
That lead to sound recourse.

I don't have to make you fit
Into my earthbound mind—
What shape or substance you may be
Is not for me to find,
To understand or even guess.
If you are Spirit or the Ghost,
I only want to feel you're here
When I need you most!

Thoughts from Inside, Spilling Over

Inspiration from the Downs

Green and verdant rolling mounds

Soft and gentle slopes of earth

Wrap around me as my birth.

'Twas disappointing some would say

Another girl to grace the day

A boy was all we hoped and sought

Another girl, it is as nought.

We have already girls to spare

No use for others

Light despair.

A lifetime later, they are gone

If only they could hear our song.

No matter now

But they were wrong.

Denny Bradbury

Mind Unburdened

Dwelling on the negative and poorly thought out way

Leads us to atrophy

Decay so immured in the mire

That all is nonsense till the light comes crashing in on fire

A ball of comprehension

So vivid in its form

It takes us to the next dimension

Leaving doubt where it should lie

Within its case of thorns.

Why try to understand the whole when nuggets will suffice?

They charge ahead transporting all who seek this different paradise.

Unburden mind

Forget the chains of those who are unable

To break the mould and freely give

Their minds to age old fable.

The Young Druid Fulfils His Destiny

Flowing robes swirled about him,

His figure muscled deep.

He stood above the crowded hill,

His flock like many sheep;

They followed him where'er he went.

His gestures grand and great,

They worshipped him.

His words of wisdom

Led them to their fate.

All engoldened with the sunrise,

A hush came o'er the throng.

He raised his arms embraced the light

They'd waited for so long.

Air throbbed with people trying

Not to cry out before time.

When all was still, expectant thrill,

He roared and sang his rhyme.

They listened to the singing voice

That rose upon the morn;

They swallowed up the rhetoric,

A hero then was born.

He spoke of love and earth and sky.

He wailed about the day

When Romans came, herded the wise,

Sought leaders whom they slay.

Sea island off the western coast

Was red with blood that moon.

Watchers wrote that 'all was well,

Dissenters dead by noon.'

While walking at his father's side

As boy he'd heard them all

The stories of their ancient ones

Who'd held the flock in thrall.

'They chased them over the mountains till they brushed against the sea,
They hounded all before them till there was no one left but thee.
Their robes they flowed around and out behind them billowing free.

As they crowded on the stormy shore, they needs must face the tide,
For all behind was danger, death from the baying men that tried
To take or break all who were against them, their feelings set aside.

Women and their children, aged old folk, too, were swept along
By the anguished need of the elders, the hitherto ruling throng—
Battle hardened foe, relentless, went and marched to a bitter song.

Those hunted down and harried, those who fled from soldiers bold
Kept up their faith, believed in what they preached from songs of old
That the ancient ones had handed down along with torques of gold.

As the sea grew dark and the storm whipped wild, over the straits they

went

To the island where they hoped and prayed that their lives would then

be spent.

They were welcomed in with fires and broth, but the signs spelt bad

portent.

As the sea stopped still and the army saw that the natives now were near,

Legions crossed the narrow sea and landed with swords and fearsome

spear.

They showed no pity as the blood lust rose with their corralled foe in fear.

Carnage it was that bitter day, with druids all slain where they stood.

Cries of the children, dying mothers, elders' pleading did no good;

Limbs and heads and torsos stained the oak trees with their blood.

It was not long before the bloody soldiers sailed for home

For pagan hoards had swept along and south and into Rome.

Sad irony that killing always, always means there's more to come.

To further shores they went to save their own beleaguered races,

For their families that were dying on their knees in sacred places.

All that met them as they journeyed back were desperate, haunted faces.

'Tis quiet now as wind and rain sweep over tracks and ancient land.

Weak summer light plays tricks, so maybe where they took their stand

Their ghosts still walk and wail until the world can understand.'

'But, Son, they didn't kill us all.

One was left who hid:

My Grandfa' saw the bloody coup

From under Stone Tilt Lid.

A special place for us it was,

For eons back in time,

Our kin had prayed and poemed,

Creating sacred rhyme.

So you see, it is our due,

Our destiny to serve.

I am old and beaten,

Now, Son, it is up to you.'

So saying, he sat down,

Face towards the sun.

He prayed and died

Atop the cliff

To wait upon death's tide.

Gleaming youth became a man

As he took up the stave.

Now he alone stood strong,

Cloaked in spirit brave.

He'd lead his people,

Teach them well.

As he fed their souls with peace,

His spell would never cease.

Water Sprite's Happy Poem

Behind the waterfall we stay

When cloud blocks out the sun.

On sunny days we laugh and sing

And splash and dance all day.

Water falling, water falling,

Rainbows dancing, dancing, dancing.

Light on light, the sun appearing,

Water Pippit flies and swoops—

Washing feathers, loops the loops.

Happy in this magic world,

He sings his song while those

About him watch in wonder

At his pure delight in this, his

Waterfall.

Water Slug maintains his pace

While washing dirt from mossy place.

He too is happy in his way

As he stops from work to play.

He settles in the shadows grey

To watch the airborne antics way

Above his head, he smiles and waves

His little tail in joyful union

With us all. For it is his, this

Waterfall.

Now Terpsichoria has come

To join the group of friends.

She is a wild and fairy thing

Who loves to dance and swirl.

Her fairy mother wished this gift

Upon her baby fair because she knew

That she would not be able to be there.

The sad and cruel world in which

She lived took her away, but now her

Lovely daughter lives and brightens up our day.

Now she will dance at everything, her feet

Are light as air as through the waterfall

She goes in and out with auburn hair

Reflecting sunshine, golden rainbows.

Safe haven for this little girl

It is now hers, the

Waterfall.

I am Water Sprite, and I say poems

In my head. Then the words that tumble out

Are better when they're said behind or in or through

The drops of water as they fall. We can't stop being who we are

That is the joy of all who live behind the

Waterfall.

Garden Nymph

She stands so still, just leaning over the trickling pond that graces the garden.

Today, she wears a snowy hat that sits so snug it almost looks as though it warms her, keeping her safe from further chill and lending an air of cosy protection so necessary in this darkest time of year.

She never moves, she merely maintains her vigil at the pond's edge looking for what?

We will never know as it is not her nature to tell, we can only guess that what she sees,

she seeks.

Jenny Wren hops doubtfully along ever wary but still she comes to join the scene Where after careful consideration, she flies to the top of the nymph and perches triumphantly.

Mistress of all she surveys she stays but a moment in case of harm her routine is quick, Bold and beautifully executed so that predators can only wonder at her next move.

Another second and she is gone to hide in the nearby conifer with cover so dense that she is safe.

Grey and white cat is outside his band of comfort and picks his way carefully through where the snow lies thinly as swept along by the erratic wind eddies and whirls, forming peaks and valleys so small that only tiny creatures appreciate the vagaries.

Grey and white cat gives up his hunting for today and carefully turns to find shelter.

He has travelled but a short distance, then a memory stirs, and he remembers that his basket is near.

Bounding careless of the pristine snow cover that begs to be left alone to glisten in Beauty, one large dog scatters all before him as he revels in the glorious new sensation. He romps, runs, shakes, and forms chaos on the snow covered lawn so closely mown in tender spirals. His nose is covered with flakes, and he looks up after failing to find the snowball. Happy canine scatters the cat and Jenny Wren back to their places of safety, but Nymph remains as still as before.

In those far-off, balmy days of summer—now so distant—with scarcely believable Warmth, we dream of snow so crisp, so clean, so magical in its transformation of the world.

Rarely do we allow the appalling reality of icy roads, deadly snow drifts with their unnecessary breakdown of society to impinge on the romantic ideal with which we toy as we swing lazily on the garden hammock. Too hot to move except to sip iced tea.

Idly do we fan the immobile face in its sweaty repose, dreaming on thoughts too vague—or even too naughty—to be shared.

Garden Nymph knows what she sees,

Looks out for frogs and such as these

Sweet smile of love with hands on knees.

Oh to have a friend like Nymph who will never give up her secrets—nor mine!

The End